THE RAILROADS THAT BUILT THE FINGER LAKES

FROM FALLEN FLAGS TO MODERN SHORT LINES

MARK KLINGEL

Fonthill Media Inc.
www.fonthillmedia.com
office@fonthillmedia.com

First published 2024

ISBN 978-1-62545-138-5

Typeset in 10pt on 13pt Sabon
Printed and bound in England

Contents

About the Author

Mark Klingel is a twenty-eight-year-old native of Southeastern Michigan who grew up in the quiet suburbs outside of Detroit, Michigan. His passion for the railroad started at the age of three, watching the Henry Ford Museum's steam locomotive, the Edison, in action. After becoming an active-duty member in the United States Coast Guard, Mark moved to Buffalo, New York, to photograph and document the railroad industry that serves America's Great Lakes and Northeastern regions.

Introduction

During the 1970s, the American railroad scene was changing rapidly, and the railroads found it difficult to adapt to the changes that were taking place. As a result of extensive government regulations, declining industrial business, and increasing competition from other modes of transportation, the freight railroad system of the United States was collapsing at an alarming rate. Even though passenger services were taken over by Amtrak beginning in 1971, many railroad companies around the country were still losing money with the idea of declaring bankruptcy looming on the horizon. In order to save the railroad industry from total collapse, the United States government formed the Consolidated Rail Corporation, also known as Conrail, as a result of President Richard Nixon signing the Regional Rail Reorganization Act of 1973 into law. This act quickly adopted the name, "3R Act." Not only did the 3R Act give birth to Conrail, it also helped form the United States Railway Association (USRA). Upon being signed into law, the USRA took over the powers of the Interstate Commerce Commission with respect to allowing the struggling and bankrupt railroads to abandon unprofitable railroad lines. The USRA was also tasked with drawing up a final system plan which would ultimately decide which rail lines would be included in Conrail.

When the final plan was unveiled in 1975, the following railroads would become assimilated into Conrail: Penn Central (Pennsylvania Railroad, New York Central, and New York, New Haven & Hartford Railroad), the Ann Arbor Railroad, Erie Lackawanna, Lehigh Valley, Reading Company, Central Railroad of New Jersey, Lehigh & Hudson River Railway, Pennsylvania-Reading Seashore Lines (merged 1976), and Monongahela Railway (merged 1993). As the years went on after the organization of Conrail, many railroad lines from the assimilated railroads were sold off and abandoned as they were no longer considered to be profitable. These same rail lines would give birth to the short line railroads you see operating throughout the state of New York with many of them tracing their origins back to Conrail and the railroads that came before it. While most of the railroads mentioned in this book trace their history back to Conrail, others trace their heritage back to other larger or even smaller railroads.

The Finger Lakes Railway, using the tracks of the New York Central, Pennsylvania, and Lehigh Valley railroads, has become a mainstay economic provider in the railroad's namesake region in upstate New York. The Livonia, Avon & Lakeville hustles food products and general freight for their growing customer base along a former Erie Lackawanna branch line between Rochester and Lakeville, NY. The Ontario Midland Railroad transports freight on the former New York Central Hojack and Pennsylvania Railroad Elmira branch lines. Operating on a leasing agreement with Norfolk Southern, the WATCO-owned Ithaca Central Railroad transports large quantities of road salt on the former route of the Lehigh Valley's famed Black Diamond using a trio of former Union Pacific EMD diesels. The Bath & Hammondsport operates old century diesel locomotives to transport freight between Painted Post, Savona, Cohoctan, and Wayland, New York, on former Erie and Delaware Lackawanna and Western tracks. The Rochester & Southern Railroad continues to operate as one of the very first railroads that became a part of the modern short line railroad conglomerate we now know today as Genesee & Wyoming Incorporated. Built from their fallen flag predecessors, these are the stories of the railroads that built the Finger Lakes region.

1

The Livonia,
Avon & Lakeville Railroad:
Rochester's Agricultural Branch Line

Headquartered in its namesake city, Lakeville, New York, the Livonia, Avon & Lakeville Railroad has been serving the agricultural communities along its 27-mile network since 1964. The railroad traces the heritage of their tracks back to the Erie Lackawanna as well as Conrail when the railroad industry was suffering immensely from new government regulations, economic changes, and financial struggles during the 1960s and 1970s. The LA&L also operates three subsidiary railroad companies: the Bath & Hammondsport Rail Corporation, the Ontario Midland Railroad, and the Western New York & Pennsylvania Railroad. While most of their right of way is former Erie Lackawanna, the railroad also operates a small former Lehigh Valley branch line to Henrietta, New York. The LA&L also maintains interchange connections with CSX and the Rochester & Southern Railroad at Genesee Junction just south of the city of Rochester.

Diving deeper into the past before the Erie Lackawanna and Conrail, the LA&L's predecessors during the 1850s were inspired by the imminent completion of the New York and Lake Erie Railroad between the Hudson River and Dunkirk on Lake Erie. In 1850, the Buffalo and Cohocton Valley Railway was incorporated to build what its backers hoped would become the Erie's route to Buffalo. The company would change its name to the Buffalo, Corning and New York Railroad in 1852 when their rail line project was nearing completion. However, before the BC&NY could finish their line to Buffalo, the only existing route between Attica and Buffalo at the time got acquired by its rival: The Buffalo and New York City Railroad. Later in 1853, the BC&NY opened their right of way between Painted Post and Caledonia, New York, with it reaching Batavia the following year. Today, the LA&L still operates this segment between Bronson Hill Road (Livonia, New York) and Avon. Another neighboring railroad, the Rochester and Genesee Valley Railroad, ran out of money in 1854 after building track between Rochester and Avon in an effort to link Rochester and Pittsburgh. Today, the LA&L operates this segment between Mortimer and Avon. Following the footsteps of the R&GV, the Genesee Valley Railroad was incorporated in 1856 with the goal to extend the R&GV from Avon to Portage through a connection with the Buffalo &

7

New York City Railroad. This company would also not last for very long either after getting sold at foreclosure in 1858 and reorganized as the Avon, Geneseo, and Mount Morris Railroad. The reorganized company officially opened the line to Mount Morris the following year. A remnant of the AG&MM survives as the LA&L's Avon industrial track that allows the railroad to serve Barilla America.

Following the GVR's connection to their tracks at Portage in 1856, the Buffalo and New York City Railroad became reorganized as the Buffalo, New York and Erie Railroad in 1857. Shortly afterward, the BNY&E acquired the recently bankrupt Buffalo, Corning and New York Railroad. The BNY&E would then go through a number of leasing agreements between 1858 and 1872. The R&GV was leased to the BNY&E in 1858 followed by the BNY&E being leased to the Erie Railroad, which was reorganized from the New York and Erie Railroad in 1861. Later in 1872, the AG&MM also became leased to the Erie. The Erie Railroad would be once again reorganized to become the New York, Lake Erie and Western Railway a few years later in 1878. The line that hosts the LA&L's Lakeville Yard and local industries was completed in 1882 by the Conesus Lake Railroad as a 1.6-mile branch from a connection with the NYLE&W at Conesus Lake Junction. This branch allowed passenger trains to meet the lake steamers of the time at a pier. Before going bankrupt in 1884, the New York, West Shore, and Buffalo Railroad completed its own rail line that ran parallel to the New York Central. Upon going bankrupt, the New York Central took control of the West Shore. The LA&L still operates 1.59 miles of the old West Shore between Mortimer and Genesee Junction. The Lehigh Valley Railroad would complete its Buffalo extension as well as its Rochester Branch in 1892, the latter of which became incorporated as a subsidiary company known as the Rochester and Honeoye Valley Railroad. The segment of the Rochester Branch between Lehigh Station Road and Mortimer is still operated by the LA&L today.

The LA&L was born when the Erie Lackawanna Railroad threatened to abandon a 13-mile branch line that reached south from Avon, connecting the neighboring towns of Lakeville and Livonia. This branch line, which also ran as far north as Industry, was known as the Erie Lackawanna's Rochester Branch. Before the Erie Lackawanna, the Rochester Division came close to abandonment between 1938 and 1941 when the Erie (reorganized back to the Erie from the NYLE&W in 1895) had gone bankrupt and reorganized under the same name. The newly reformed Erie cut back passenger service to a single pair of mixed trains with doodlebugs being utilized occasionally between Avon and Corning during the early 1940s. The Erie would maintain this routine until 1947 when management decided to end passenger services on the line. Freight service continued into the early 1950s with one train operating each way daily due to a noticeable decline in freight traffic. Giving birth to the "Livonia-Lakeville Spur" in 1956, the Rochester Division was abandoned between the north side of Wayland and Livonia. A few years later in 1960, the Erie and the Delaware, Lackawanna and Western Railroads merged to form the Erie Lackawanna. When the Erie Lackawanna announced their plans to abandon the line, the Livonia community stepped in to save the railroad. Led by local bank president, Chester Haak, and a number of LA&L founders, the Livonia community purchased the dying branch line for $13,000 in 1964. The LA&L originally started out as a tourist railroad but began offering freight service some time later. The community of Livonia would lose its rail service connection in 1981 due to the State of New York's desire to avoid replacing an overpass that carried Bronson Hill Road over the LA&L's right of way. The tracks between Bronson Hill Road and Livonia were promptly abandoned and the LA&L's team track in Lakeville was built to service customers in the Lakeville area.

Starting in 1976, the LA&L's main interchange railroad in Avon became Conrail instead of the Erie Lackawanna. The railroad would continue to interchange with Conrail until 1995 when Conrail announced its desire to sell off its branches to smaller railroad companies who would be able to provide better rail service to their customers. The LA&L quickly jumped at the chance to expand its railroad and purchased the Conrail Mortimer Secondary and the Rochester Industrial Track for an undisclosed sum that same year. This new expansion allowed the LA&L to service customers in Avon and Henrietta with direct access to Genesee Junction. The expansion also eliminated the need for an overhead Conrail move from Henrietta to Avon. The LA&L's purchase of track from Conrail added 18.5 miles to their network. As a result of this expansion, the LA&L's total length reached up to 27 miles.

Today, the LA&L has become one of the better-known short line railroads in the state of New York. Among railfans and enthusiasts, the railroad is widely recognized as one of the many short line railroads operating a full roster of ALCO diesel locomotives on its own rails as well as its subsidiaries.

Beginning the northbound journey to Rochester, LA&L 420, 428, and 425 put on a show of smoke and exhaust. The engineer throttles up all three Alco diesel units to get the train over the uphill grade out of Lakeville yard.

The LA&L's current customer and traffic base is mostly based around food products such as grains, corn, syrups, fertilizer, beans, agricultural products, food products, sweeteners, and lumber.

The LA&L employs "Century" type diesels which were a series of road switchers built in a variety of models during the 1960s. The LA&L's roster of Century diesels consists of models such as C420s, C424s, C425s, and C430s.

Scenic highlights on the LA&L's route include the railroad bridge at Pole Bridge Road, Avon Depot, the Avon Barilla Factory, the Rochester & Genesee Valley Railroad passenger depot and museum grounds in Industry, and the railroad bridge crossing the Genesee River in Rochester.

Crossing over the Genesee River in Rochester, the northbound LA&L road train approaches the railroad's interchange point with CSX and Rochester & Southern known as Genesee Junction. The LA&L's tracks run directly parallel to the CSX West Shore Subdivision between Genesee Junction and Red Creek.

The depot in Industry that is now part of the Rochester & Genesee Valley Railroad Museum is one of the main photo locations on their line between Rochester and Lakeville.

After delivering a line of hopper cars to Howlett Farms, the southbound LA&L road train eases its way past milepost 367 before switching the yard in Avon.

Like its neighboring short line railroads in the region, the LA&L has done its best to preserve rail service over lines that would have been abandoned had they not stepped in.

Continuing their journey back to Lakeville, LA&L 425 leads the southbound road train past the Rochester & Genesee Valley Railroad Museum at golden hour.

In 1998, the LA&L bought a controlling share in the 14-mile-long Ontario Central Railroad between Victor and Shortsville. The LA&L's controlling interests in the Ontario Central were sold to the Finger Lakes Railway in 2007. As of 2022, the old Ontario Central's tracks between Victor and Manchester have been deemed out of service.

The former Erie Railroad depot in Avon is now home to a local restaurant known as Duffy's Tavern.

Splitting off from the CSX West Shore Subdivision at Red Creek, the LA&L road train turns south to deliver freight traffic to Avon and Lakeville.

Today, the LA&L follows a route through Lakeville, Avon, Rush, and Henrietta at Mortimer Junction. From there the route continues west to Genesee Junction on track that runs parallel to the CSX West Shore Branch. The LA&L's line also runs southeast to West Henrietta on the former Lehigh Valley Rochester Branch.

The LA&L also operated other ALCO diesel switchers such as LA&L RS-1 no. 20, the first ALCO diesel that was acquired by the railroad. No. 20 joined the LA&L's roster in 1972. After working on the LA&L for several years, the old RS-1 was relegated to work trains and yard switching duty in Lakeville in the 1990s.

No. 20 was donated and delivered to the Rochester & Genesee Valley Railroad Museum of Rush, New York, in 2016 after spending almost a decade in storage. LA&L no. 20 now operates at the museum, giving rides to tourists on the museum grounds that are situated directly next to the LA&L's mainline.

Heading back to Midway on the museum grounds, SEPTA interurban car 161 rounds the bend at Giles during the evening golden hour at the Trains & Trolleys at Twilight event. The New York Museum of Transportation and the Rochester & Genesee Valley Railroad Museum share a small branch line that connects with the LA&L at Industry and loops around the NYMOT grounds.

U.S. Army 1843 is a Fairbanks Morse H12-44 diesel locomotive that served at the Seneca Army depot in Romulus, New York, until 1993. During its time at the Seneca Army depot, it handled approximately 30 to 100 cars per week on the 42 miles of track inside of the army base. Today, a part of the old Seneca Army base is now used by the Finger Lakes Railway for freight car storage.

Lehigh Valley 211 is an Alco RS-3 that was built for the Pennsylvania Railroad in 1953. It is the only survivor of a small group RS-3's built with a high short hood to house the dynamic brakes and a steam generator used to heat passenger cars. The 211 spent approximately one year working in revenue service on the Rochester & Southern Railroad on a lease agreement before enjoying its new life in preservation.

Rochester Gas & Electric 1941 had a very brief career on the LA&L between 1964 and 1965. LA&L sold the switcher to RG&E in 1965 and the small center cab switcher was later donated to the Rochester & Genesee Valley Railroad Museum by RG&E in 1991. Here we see 1941 posing with museum personnel during a night photo session in August 2021.

Rochester & Genesee Valley Railroad Museum personnel pose with their recently restored Lehigh Valley caboose for photographers during a night photo session hosted by the museum.

RG&E 1941 and museum staff pose for photographers in order to recreate a scene from the past: working as an industrial switcher for Rochester Gas & Electric.

2

Finger Lakes Railway: The Railroad That Revived a Fallen Flag

The Finger Lakes region, an area in upstate New York comprised of small villages and cities situated along a series of lakes whose shapes closely resemble the fingers on a human hand, is well known for its spectacular scenery. The region is also home to one of the most widely recognized short line railroads in New York: The Finger Lakes Railway (FGLK). In a region that is notably rich with short lines powered by high horsepower Alcos, the Finger Lakes Railway is famous for providing railroad services to its namesake region using EMD GP38-2s and General Electric B23-7s dressed in the colors of the New York Central Railroad. The New York Central livery, along with their mixed roster, gives railroad enthusiasts the rare and unique opportunity to shoot the vintage fallen flag paint scheme on home rails. The same can be said for their sole Lehigh Valley painted unit: FGLK U23B no. 2201. Based out of Geneva, New York, in the heart of its namesake region, the Finger Lakes Railway operates 167 miles of former New York Central, Lehigh Valley, and Pennsylvania Railroad track between Geneva, Auburn, Solvay, Himrod, Watkins Glen, Victor, Penn Yan, and Canandaigua. The Finger Lakes Railway was founded in 1995 when the railroad purchased Conrail's Geneva Cluster. The Geneva Cluster consisted of the remains of the New York Central's Auburn Road, sections of the Pennsylvania Railroad's Elmira Branch, and sections of the Lehigh Valley's Buffalo Division mainline. Between the railroad's predecessors and its chosen primary paint scheme, the Finger Lakes Railway can be considered as the railroad that revived a fallen flag.

The New York Central's Auburn Road is regarded as one of the oldest active railroad lines in America and was completed in 1839 following the founding of the Auburn & Syracuse Railroad in 1834. The A&S extended between Syracuse and Rochester and passed through the towns of Geneva and Canandaigua. The A&S was a part of the first railroad line to stretch from Albany to Buffalo. Another railroad, the Auburn & Rochester Railroad, was chartered in 1836 with its construction completed to the Auburn & Syracuse in November 1841. The 104 miles of track connected the city of Rochester to Victor, Canandaigua, Shortsville, Clifton Springs, Phelps, Geneva, Waterloo, Seneca Falls, Cayuga, Auburn, Skaneateles Junction, Marcellus, Camillus,

Solvay, and Syracuse. With the completion of other neighboring short line railroads by 1843, residents of the area were finally able to travel west to Niagara Falls and east to Albany with relative ease. In 1850, the two neighboring railroads consolidated to become the Rochester & Syracuse Railroad and quickly began work on building a new and more direct mainline between the two cities. The New York Central Railroad was born that same year when the Rochester & Syracuse merged with seven other short line railroads that were operating between Albany and Buffalo. Erastus Corning, an industrialist from Albany, orchestrated the merger and became its first company president when the merger was complete. Thanks to the amount of political power he held at the time, he was able to overcome dissent in New York's State Legislature by numerous investors in the canal system. The New York Central Railroad changed forever in 1867 when Cornelius Vanderbilt, known to many as "The Commodore," acquired control of the railroad with the intent of merging the New York Central with his Hudson River Railroad. Vanderbilt successfully merged the two companies into the New York Central and Hudson River Railroad in 1869. With this new railroad company, Vanderbilt controlled one of the first giant corporations in America's history. The mainline ran from New York City to Albany, Buffalo, and Niagara Falls with the Auburn Road becoming a thriving branch line.

From 1853 until the mid-1900s, the Auburn Road served as a through route that saw a large amount of passenger and freight traffic respectively. Many freight trains served a large variety of local industries and nearly every town or city that was being served by the Auburn Road had its own freight depot, some of which are still standing today along the modern Finger Lakes Railway right of way. The New York Central and Hudson River would change their company name back to the New York Central in 1914 with prosperity on the Auburn Road still booming as total miles of track and patronage were nearing peak levels. The Auburn Road connected with two independent short line railroads at Marcellus and Skaneateles Junction. The Marcellus & Otisco Lake Railway diverged from the New York Central in Martisco and ran to the village and lake known as Otisco. To avoid any confusion of having two stations named Marcellus, the New York Central changed the name of its own station to Martisco. At Skaneateles Junction, the New York Central connected with the Skaneateles Short Line Railroad, which ran to its namesake village of Skaneateles. The New York Central Auburn Road also crossed and connected with its archrival, the Pennsylvania Railroad, at Phelps Junction and Canandaigua, as well as the Lehigh Valley at Auburn, Cayuga, Geneva, Shortsville, and Fishers.

Railroad usage on the Auburn Road began to decline after World War II with the introduction of the interstate highway system. Passenger services ended by 1958, and the New York Central abandoned the Auburn Road's tracks between Victor and Pittsford. Like many railroads of the time, the New York Central was suffering from the economic and industrial changes happening in America. The New York Central began looking to the possibility of merging with another railroad company in order to improve their situation. Such railroads that the New York Central courted were the Baltimore & Ohio and the Chesapeake & Ohio. However, these merger talks between the three railroads would not last long. Merger talks abruptly ended when feuds broke out between the leaders of the three railroads regarding who would head the new company if any kind of merger took place between them. With the prospect of merging with the

B&O or the C&O now out the window, the New York Central began official talks with the Pennsylvania Railroad. These talks between the two notorious archrivals began in October 1961 and would continue for the next few years until January 1968 when the Interstate Commerce Commission approved the merger in a surprise move. This merger would give birth to one of the largest corporate failures in America's history: The Penn Central Railroad.

The Penn Central Transportation Company was launched in February of 1968 and was unfortunately doomed since day one of operations. The Penn Central would succumb to bankruptcy in June 1970 and the Auburn Road suffered immensely between the tracks being in bad condition and derailments that became increasingly more common. The Penn Central would become absorbed into the Consolidated Rail Corporation/ Conrail in April 1976. Under Conrail, the Lehigh Valley's once bustling mainline to Buffalo became silent and the right of way from Canandaigua to Victor and from Pittsford to Rochester became abandoned by 1982. Going into the 1990s, Conrail only used the Auburn Road from Auburn to Solvay. The Finger Lakes Railway Corporation stepped in to purchase the Auburn Road in 1995 with the tracks being rebuilt and new customers being added over time. Thanks to the hard work of the Finger Lakes Railway, one of the oldest active railroad lines in the United States is enjoying a new lease on life as part of a thriving modern short line railroad.

Most of the Finger Lakes Railway operations take place on the former New York Central's Auburn Road between Canandaigua, Geneva, Auburn, and Solvay, New York. The primary road train known as GS2 handles the freight traffic between Geneva, Auburn, and Solvay, while the GC2 job is responsible for traffic between Geneva and Canandaigua, New York, with as-needed trips up the old Lehigh Valley to Manchester.

Finger Lakes B23-7 2301 crosses over Gates Avenue in Geneva on the GY1 job. 2301 wears a commemorative nameplate for John R. Sullivan, a veteran of the Boston & Maine Railroad and a former Marketing Director of FGLK.

Geneva is the Finger Lakes Railway's interchange point with Norfolk Southern. Norfolk Southern operates H06 as an interchange job via its Corning Secondary from Gang Mills to Geneva approximately six days per week. FGLK also interchanges with CSX in Solvay which calls for GS2 to run daily, except Saturdays, in order to pick up and drop off freight cars in Auburn as well as to interchange traffic going to and from CSX.

During the early evening hours, the Finger Lakes GS2 train eases its way through Seneca Falls westbound while passing by the old New York Central passenger depot.

The Skaneateles Short Line Railroad connected with the New York Central at Skaneateles Junction. Originally built as the Skaneateles & Jordan Railroad from 1836 to 1850, the small railroad served more than a dozen industries from 1836 to 1981.

Heading westbound through Shortsville on the Auburn Road, GP38-2 2002 leads the GC2 job past milepost 69 with a line of covered hoppers in tow. These hoppers would be delivered to the Pactiv Corporation located at the current end of the line.

Working the AY1 local in Auburn, B23-7 2305 prepares to shove a line of mill gondolas under the crane to be loaded with products from Nucor Steel Company.

Heading to the east end of Geneva on the GY2 local, GMTX 232, an MP15E diesel switcher, leads a pair of covered hopper cars to Blowers Agra Service.

Finger Lakes U23B 2201 passes by an abandoned mill while leading the westbound GS2 train through Auburn during the summer of 2021. By the summer of 2022, this mill would later be demolished.

GMTX 396 switches the yard in Solvay in preparation for the departure of the westbound GS2 train.

Preparing to depart Geneva, Norfolk Southern train H06 waits patiently for Finger Lakes GY2 to position a small cut of covered hopper cars to be attached to the awaiting southbound NS train. The hoppers were loaded with grain at DeLong Company in Geneva before being picked up by GY2 earlier that same morning.

After switching DeLong Company at the north end of Geneva, Finger Lakes 2201 leads the GY1 job and a line of covered hoppers back to Geneva Yard.

The GC2 job prepares to switch Phelps Junction.

At the east side of Canandaigua, the Finger Lakes Railway utilizes a siding to store hoppers to be delivered to the Pactiv Corporation at the end of their line. Here we see the eastbound GC2 slowly depart Canandaigua after completing their work at Pactiv.

Departing Solvay westbound, a trio of EMD GP38-2s lead the GS2 train out of town while passing a New York Central-era semaphore signal.

The Finger Lakes Railway also operates on sections of the Lehigh Valley's mainline to Buffalo between Kendaia and Geneva as well as Shortsville to Victor. Chartered in 1846 to transport anthracite coal from the coal fields of Pennsylvania, the Lehigh Valley Railroad grew into a freight and passenger carrier between Jersey City, New Jersey, and Buffalo, New York. The Lehigh Valley Railroad first connected to the Finger Lakes region in 1871 when the railroad financed the Southern Central Railroad to complete a coal hauling railroad line from Athens, Pennsylvania, to North Fair Haven on Lake Ontario via the towns of Owego and Auburn. Five years later in 1876, the Lehigh Valley took control of the Geneva, Ithaca, and Sayre Railroad which provided the Lehigh Valley with a means to build their own mainline to Buffalo. Despite this, the railroad ran into the issue of tackling the steep grades out of Ithaca, which proved to be too steep for heavy freight trains to travel on. To solve this issue, the railroad opened up a new route from Van Etten to Geneva in 1892 to bypass these steep uphill grades. This railroad line was also completed from Geneva to Buffalo. With the bypass now open, the original route through Ithaca became used for passenger trains and smaller local freights and a large freight yard and locomotive servicing facility was built in Manchester on the new route from Geneva to Buffalo that same year. Once recognized as the largest railroad yard in the world, the Lehigh Valley's facility in Manchester employed more than 1,000 people during the peak of its operations. Manchester Yard would finally close its doors in 1970 as a result of rapidly declining freight traffic.

The Lehigh Valley built and acquired a multitude of railroad lines in upstate New York during the early 1900s. These new feeder lines included connections to Cayuga Lake, Auburn, Canada via Niagara Falls, Geneva, Rochester, Hemlock Lake, Elmira and Oneida Lake via East Ithaca, Cortland, and Canastota. The Lehigh Valley also joined with the New York Central's Auburn Road at LV Junction to cross Cayuga Lake. Despite being a coal hauling railroad, the Lehigh Valley was widely recognized for the passenger services the railroad provided. Geneva and Ithaca boasted busy passenger stations with name trains such as the Maple Leaf and the Star traveling through the Finger Lakes region, including the Lehigh Valley's premier passenger train: The Black Diamond Express. Running from New York City to Buffalo, the Black Diamond was promoted and advertised as a train of luxury and the fastest in the Lehigh Valley's fleet. The Black Diamond had all the necessities and amenities anyone riding the train could dream of or want from plush velvet chairs, skilled chefs, and much more. Initially called "The Handsomest Train in the World" by the Lehigh Valley, the roadbed and tracks it traveled on quickly became known as "The Route of the Black Diamond." The Black Diamond also adopted the nickname, "The Honeymoon Express," due to the appeal of newlyweds who rode the train on their way to Niagara Falls.

The end of the Lehigh Valley began after World War II as the railroads began to struggle to keep themselves afloat. As train traffic and revenue continued to decrease, the tracks also began to disappear as fast as the trains did. Passenger services ended between Ithaca and Auburn in 1948 and the Black Diamond and the Star made their final runs on May 11, 1959. The Maple Leaf made its last run into Geneva in February of 1961 during the midst of a heavy snowstorm. The following year in 1962, the Pennsylvania Railroad assumed control of the Lehigh Valley. With passenger services gone, the tracks from Ithaca to Geneva were torn up in 1963 and the double track mainline became a single track sometime later in the mid-1960s. The Lehigh Valley officially went bankrupt in 1970, with the only operating portions of the railroad left in the Finger Lakes being the mainline to Buffalo via Geneva and a small handful of branch lines. Like the other dying railroads of the time, the Lehigh Valley was absorbed into Conrail on April 1, 1976. Under Conrail, most of the Black Diamond route was shut down and removed by the end of the 1970s. As of 2022, the tracks between Victor and Manchester have been deemed out of service. The Route of the Black Diamond may be a far cry from what it once was, but the Finger Lakes Railway has kept the small remaining remnants alive as a small short line railroad in upstate New York.

The Shortsville to Victor section splits off from the former New York Central at Shortsville and continues west through the town of Manchester before ending at the industrial sidings of Victor Insulators. In Manchester, one can visit the Finger Lakes Railway Park which has pieces of Lehigh Valley railroad equipment on display. The Finger Lakes Railway Park is currently the home of a Lehigh Valley bay window caboose, two Lehigh Valley boxcars, and a searchlight signal situated in the center of the small rail park.

If a rail enthusiast is lucky enough, they will see Finger Lakes Railway U23B no. 2201 working the GC2 and GK2 jobs on the former Lehigh Valley mainline dressed in its Lehigh Valley inspired paint scheme.

The Finger Lakes Railway operates the GK2 job between Geneva and Kendaia on their southernmost section of the remnants of the Lehigh Valley. The tracks turn off the New York Central at the east end of the Finger Lakes main yard in Geneva and follow the shoreline of Seneca Lake to the old Seneca Army Depot that is now used by the railroad to store freight cars for customers. The former Seneca Army Depot occupied more than 10,000 acres of land and was used as a munitions storage and disposal facility by the United States Army from 1941 until 2000.

While not much remains of this former Lehigh Valley mainline, an old signal bridge still stands over the right of way in Geneva and an old Lehigh Valley searchlight signal also remains near the south end of the line in Kendaia.

At the southwest end of the region between Himrod, Watkins Glen, and occasionally Penn Yan, the Finger Lakes Railway operates revenue freight trains on the former Pennsylvania Railroad's Elmira Branch. Before the former Pennsylvania Railroad right of way became the coal hauling Elmira Branch, its origins date back to the mid-1840s as the Canandaigua and Corning Railroad. The capital that was to be raised totaled out to be $1,600,000 when the railroad was officially incorporated in 1845. A committee consisting of J. M. Wheeler, M. H. Sibley, Jared Wilson, John A. Granger, and Oliver Phelps was appointed to submit a favorable report with another committee also being appointed to obtain a survey of the planned route. By the time the engineer, Marvin Porter, had completed his work in July 1845, the total cost to build the railroad was estimated to cost $950,100. After multiple meetings were held over the course of a few years, the railroad broke ground at Penn Yan on July 4, 1850, and was making full headway by the following year. Approximately one thousand men were employed on building track from Penn Yan to Jefferson (now Watkins Glen) with grading underway near Canandaigua. The railroad officially opened between Canandaigua to Watkins Glen in September 1851 with the first train making its run over the road in two hours time on September 15. For a period of time, the New York & Erie Railroad provided railroad equipment for a specified rate per mile. Marvin Porter, the railroad's engineer, was named the first superintendent and three trains were run in each direction on a daily basis. The railroad connected with the Chemung Railroad at Watkins Glen and the Chemung Railroad remained under control of the New York & Erie for an indefinite period. On the Chemung, two passenger trains and two freight trains made the regular round trip daily. In 1852, the Canandaigua & Corning changed their name to the Canandaigua and Elmira Railroad and the railroad began running their own trains the following year after purchasing six locomotives and a sufficient number of rolling stock.

The Canandaigua & Elmira Railroad was sold to parties in Elmira and Penn Yan, New York, as well as Providence, Rhode Island, in 1857. Under the new ownership, the name was changed to the Canandaigua and Niagara Falls Railroad before being leased to the Erie Railroad in 1859. The Northern Central Railroad would assume this lease in 1866 but would assume full control in 1872 when the lease got cancelled. As part of the Northern Central, its main terminus became Canandaigua. The Northern Central was also a part of the Pennsylvania Railroad System, and all railroad lines north of Elmira were formally taken over by the Pennsylvania Railroad in 1911. Originally, Stanley Station was called Gorham Station. The station got its name in the early 1900s when an old oil can was found in the Pennsylvania Railroad depot bearing the name that was Gorham Station. In order to avoid any confusion with another station bearing the same name on the Middlesex Valley Railroad, Gorham Station was renamed to Stanley in honor of Seth Stanley. Seth Stanley was honored in that he gave certain grants of land and right of way through the village of Stanley for the railroad. The Elmira Branch was also a relatively popular excursion line as many tourists rode the trains to the Finger Lakes region during the summer season.

The Pennsylvania Railroad was no exception when it came to the railroads of America struggling to survive in the latter half of the twentieth century. On the Elmira Branch in particular, the use of coal quickly declined as industries around Lake Ontario began converting their facilities to use other sources of fuel and energy. As the number of passengers riding the trains decreased, so did the revenue the passenger trains generated for the railroad. At times there were more crewmen on the train than passengers due to

New York State's railway labor laws requiring full crews on trains. Each train required an engineer, fireman, and conductor no matter how small the train was.

The fate of passenger travel on the Elmira branch was sealed in 1955 when the railroad posted train-off notices at every station stop and asked the New York State Public Service Commission permission to abandon all passenger trains on the line. The trains included were the northbound train no. 595 from Williamsport to Canandaigua and train no. 596 from Canandaigua to Williamsport. Both of these trains stopped in Penn Yan daily. The last passenger trains ran through Penn Yan on January 2, 1956, with little to no fanfare in the midst of the winter weather gripping the region at the time. The original last runs were scheduled for September 25, 1955, but two lawsuits that were filed postponed passenger service abandonment until January 3, 1956. On the evening of January 2, 1956, train no. 596, consisting of one diesel locomotive, a baggage car, and a single passenger coach, rolled into Penn Yan for the last time. On board the train were eleven passengers, plus the standard train crew. The conductor made the final call to board the train at Penn Yan and the train departed shortly after. Train no. 596 with its single passenger coach rolled across the trestle over the outlet and disappeared into the darkness of the pitch-black night for the final time.

While no longer the Pennsylvania Railroad, the modern Finger Lakes Railway has kept the old branch line active hauling grain, plastics, salt, and other raw materials to various points outside of the region. Even though the Finger Lakes predecessors are now long gone, it is fair to say that this short line railroad with its unique paint schemes and customer service has helped revive these fallen flags.

Unlike Watkins Glen, Penn Yan is a smaller and much quieter village holding onto its rural Mennonite roots. Here we find the HW2 job preparing to depart Penn Yan for the southbound journey back to Himrod.

Despite Watkins Glen's lakeside appeal, many rail enthusiasts flock to the north end between Himrod and Penn Yan, hoping to catch a train slowly dragging a small line of covered hoppers through the gorgeous farm country around Penn Yan.

Despite the modern two-lane blacktop in the surrounding areas, it is not uncommon to see horse and buggies trotting along the back roads of Himrod and Penn Yan. The right of way from Penn Yan to Watkins Glen is now so quiet and scenic that it can be hard to believe that it was once one of the Pennsylvania Railroad's main coal hauling routes from the mines in Pennsylvania to the loading docks of Sodus Bay at Lake Ontario.

As the sun rises in the rural countryside, GP38-2's 2002 and 2003 lead a trio of hoppers northbound out of Himrod to Penn Yan. In this short consist, two of the hoppers were to be delivered to Silgan Plastics, and one hopper was bound for Birkett Mills.

Cargill Salt is one of two active customers that are served by the Finger Lakes HW2 job at the south end of what remains of the PRR Elmira Branch.

Finger Lakes B23-7's 1943 and 2309 bring in the southbound HG2 from Geneva into Himrod yard. Finger Lakes Railway operates this train twice a week between Himrod and Geneva via Norfolk Southern's Corning Secondary in order to transport freight traffic to and from this part of the Finger Lakes network.

Finger Lakes B23-7 2304 switches out U.S. Salt during a routine trip to Watkins Glen.

Right: To rail enthusiasts and photographers, the Finger Lakes Railway traverses through some of the most scenic parts of the region. The tracks in Watkins Glen allow trains to wind their way along the shoreline of Seneca Lake, and trains can be commonly seen working U.S. Salt and Cargill with downtown Watkins Glen nestled between the two major industries.

Below: Running light power back to Himrod from Penn Yan, Finger Lakes B23-7's 2306 and 2310 slowly ease their way through the rural New York farm country. This would be 2306's final trip to Penn Yan as the old diesel locomotive would become involved in a derailment near Himrod Yard only a few days later. This derailment would put the 2306 out of service permanently.

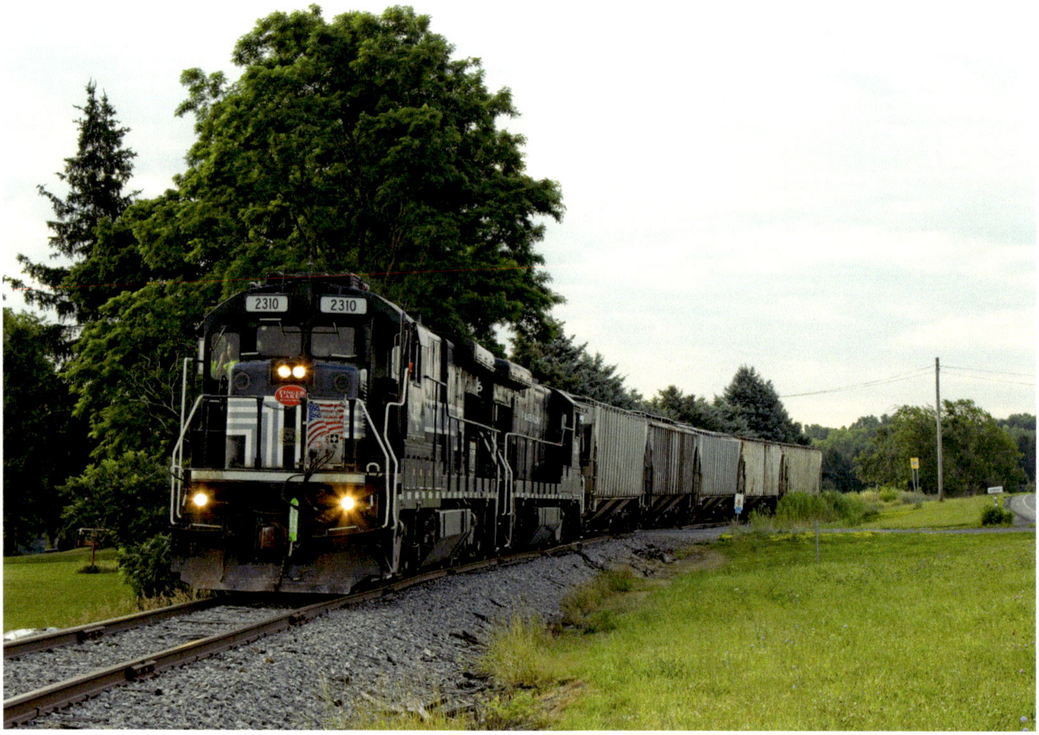
2310
2310

SENECA LAKE CRUISES
TICKETS
1943
1943

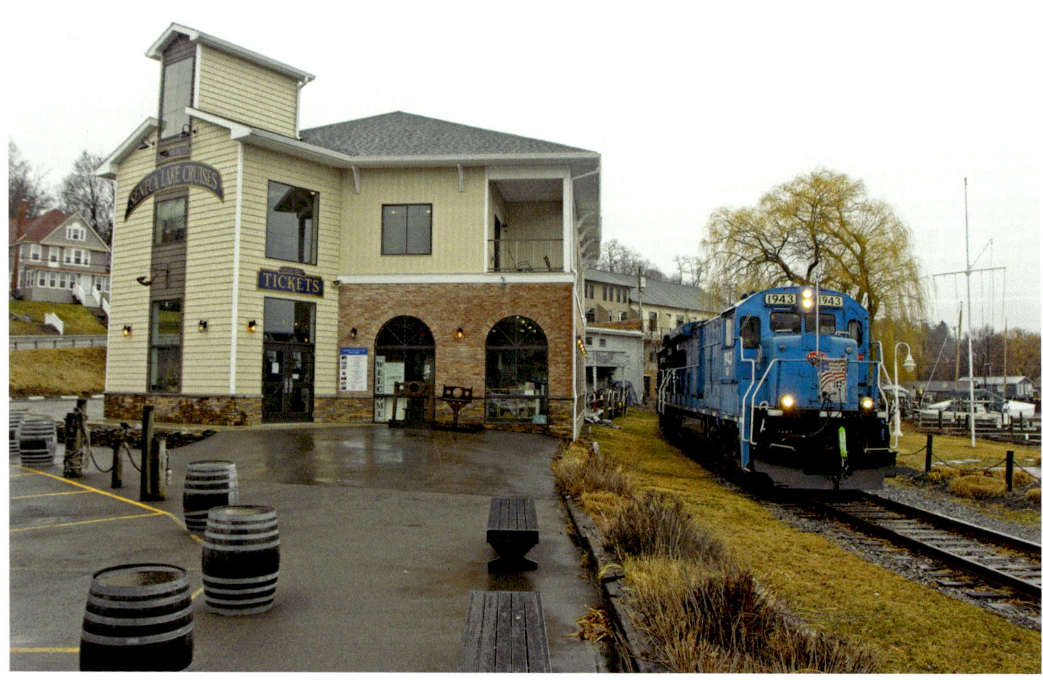

Finger Lakes 1943 pauses briefly before reversing back to Cargill to begin the regular switching manoeuvres.

Opposite above: Leading the way to Penn Yan, 2310 and 2306 slowly drag five covered hopper cars northbound to be delivered to Birkett Mills.

Opposite below: After switching U.S. Salt, the HW2 job eases its way along the Watkins Glen shoreline at the south end of Seneca Lake. The next customer on their schedule is Cargill Salt, located at the end of the line.

3

Ithaca Central:
The Salt Road of the Southern Tier

Of all the short line railroads operating in New York State, the youngest of them all is the Watco-owned Ithaca Central Railroad. Located deep in New York's Southern Tier, the Ithaca Central Railroad has tapped into the road salt market using approximately 48 miles of a former Lehigh Valley branch line between Lansing, New York, and Sayre, Pennsylvania. The Ithaca Central began operations in December 2018 after signing a leasing agreement with Norfolk Southern, which was looking for another railroad to assume control of operations on the old branch. The railroad's main customer is the Cargill Salt Mine, which is located about 5 miles north of Ithaca on the southeastern shoreline of one of the Finger Lakes, Cayuga Lake. While the salt mine in Watkins Glen transports table salt via the Finger Lakes Railway, the mine in Lansing transports road salt via the Ithaca Central. With Cargill being the railroad's main customer, almost all the Ithaca Central's freight traffic is road salt and brine. The railroad also serves another smaller customer, a pipe supplier known as ADS, in Waverly, New York, just north of Sayre. To haul these bulk cargos, Watco employs a trio of former Union Pacific SD40-2s dating back to 1969 and 1971. Two of these diesel locomotives, 4247 and 4248, still sport their Union Pacific paint with the Ithaca Central and Watco decals.

Like the Pennsylvania Railroad and the New York Central, the Lehigh Valley would build their mainline and multiple branch lines throughout the Finger Lakes region from the middle of the 1800s up until the early 1960s. The Geneva and Ithaca Railroad Company was incorporated in 1870 in order to build the first railroad to connect its namesake cities. When the G&I opened in 1873, the line connected with the New York Central's Auburn Road in Geneva and the Ithaca and Athens Branch Railroad in Ithaca, which operated south towards the Pennsylvania state line near Sayre. For the Geneva and Ithaca Railroad, everything seemed to be starting off well for them following the testing of the Taughnanock Creek railroad bridge in July of that same year. However, the joy of the completion of the railroad was short lived. In September 1873, the Geneva and Ithaca Railroad got caught up in the nationwide financial collapse that became known as the Panic of 1873. With the railroad being unable to pay its bills, a bankruptcy sale quickly followed with the Lehigh Valley purchasing the railroad line for $50,000. With the Lehigh Valley now the owners of the bankrupt Geneva and Ithaca Railroad, the line was extended to Sayre, Pennsylvania, and became known as the Lehigh Valley's Ithaca Branch.

Following the purchase of the branch by the Lehigh Valley, the Ithaca Branch thrived as one of the railroad's main arteries in the region. The Lehigh Valley carried many inbound shipments of furniture, farm machinery, lumber, fuel, food, and many more everyday commodities while outbound shipments consisted of grain, hay, and grapes. The Lehigh Valley opened the new trunk line from Van Etten to Geneva in 1892 which connected in Geneva with the main line to Buffalo as well as the route to Sayre. This new rail line allowed trains to traverse through the Finger Lakes region along the east side of Seneca Lake which helped heavy freight trains bypass the steep grades going down into Ithaca and going up out of Ithaca. Today, remnants of the route from Van Etten to Geneva are operated by the Finger Lakes Railway between Geneva and Kendaia.

The peak years for service on the Ithaca Branch would begin to end after 1918. By that time the automobile and the roads they traveled on were becoming the next major means of transportation on land and the railroads began to struggle to compete in terms of time of service and convenience. Local passenger train service ended in 1949 and the last through trains from Geneva to Sayre finally ended in 1961. In a 1961 article, the *Interlaken Review* provided a tribute to the end of the railroad when it stated, "The days of the Black Diamond, the fast express trains, the noisy little milk trains, the smoky steamers, with the exception of the powerful diesels, are at an end. And somehow—for all their noise—the smoke and whistles that split the night, we are sorry to see them go. We shall remember and admire them for the tremendous tasks they performed and how they helped link village with city and east with west and of the good will they dispatched at every stop in between." While the days of the Black Diamond have long since passed, the remains of the Lehigh Valley's Ithaca Branch are still being kept active hauling large quantities of salt to help towns and cities fight off the winter weather in various parts of the United States.

Left: The Ithaca Central Railroad's logo as seen from the side of one of their diesel locomotives.

Below: The basic operations of the Ithaca Central consist of running covered hoppers and tank cars between the Cargill Cayuga Salt Mine and the Norfolk Southern interchange in Sayre, Pennsylvania. Hoppers loaded with road salt and empty tank cars are transported south to Sayre to be interchanged with Norfolk Southern. After making the drop off in Sayre, empty hoppers and tank cars loaded with brine are taken back north to the Cargill Salt Mine.

Right: Ithaca Central's trio of SD40M-2s battle the steep uphill grade out of Ithaca at Station Road with a long line of loaded hoppers bound for the interchange in Sayre.

Below: The southbound road train arrives at Sayre Yard after receiving permission from Norfolk Southern. The Ithaca Central crew begins to ease the train towards the south end of the yard before picking up the hoppers on the adjacent siding to take back north to Ithaca.

The route of the Ithaca Central passes through the communities of Lansing, Ithaca, Newfield, West Danby, Spencer, Van Etten, Lockwood, and Waverly before ending at the Norfolk Southern interchange in Sayre. The route provides rail enthusiasts a great opportunity to explore the rural and somewhat mountainous countryside of New York's Southern Tier.

Due to the demand of road salt being at its peak when snow and ice are present, the busy season for the Ithaca Central is during the winter.

Quickly picking up speed to get a running start out of Ithaca, Ithaca Central's SD40M-2s prepare for the uphill battle to Spencer as they continue to follow the Cayuga Inlet that closely parallels the former Lehigh Valley branch line.

The southbound road train coasts downhill into Spencer. Spencer is considered to be the halfway point on the line between Ithaca and Sayre.

Van Etten is where the Lehigh Valley's trunk line to Geneva split off from the Ithaca Branch. In the modern present, however, this junction is no longer present.

Heading downhill towards Ithaca, the northbound road train rounds the bend at Station Road.

The southbound road train rolls through Lockwood with the mountains of New York's Southern Tier overlooking the valley. Lockwood is a very notable location for photographers when fall color is in full swing.

The Ithaca Central employs a trio of EMD SD40-2s (4248, 4241, and 4247). While 4248 and 4247 both originally hail from the Southern Pacific and Union Pacific Railroads, 4241 was originally built as a GP7 for the Santa Fe before being rebuilt as a SD40M-2.

Above: The southbound road train reduces speed as they approach Waverly and Sayre Yard.

Left: Rounding the bend in Van Etten, Ithaca Central 4247 leads the northbound train back to Ithaca.

Ithaca Central 4247 passes by an old wooden barn located just south of Ithaca.

The Ithaca Central road train rolls past the Shepard Creek Chapel after departing Sayre with empty hoppers bound for the mine in Lansing.

Ithaca Central 4247 leads the northbound road train through Spencer, New York, at milepost 289.

GMTX 74 is an EMD SW1001 that serves as the yard and shop switcher for UTC Railcar Repair Services in Sayre. This switcher currently spends its days marshalling freight cars between the shop buildings and sidings in Sayre Yard for maintenance and repairs.

Sayre, Pennsylvania, is the interchange point between Ithaca Central and Norfolk Southern. Nowadays, the train activity in Sayre is a far cry from what it once was compared to when the yard was under ownership of the Lehigh Valley Railroad.

After crossing the state line back into New York, Ithaca Central 4247 leads the northbound road train back to Ithaca in the midst of wintertime rain showers.

4

The Ontario Midland Railway: LA&L's Newest Family Member

Operating on 47 miles of track in Monroe and Wayne counties of New York State since 1979, the Ontario Midland is another short line railroad that employs ALCO diesel locomotives to service its customers and interchange with CSX. Operating under the reporting mark known as OMID, the railroad serves fruit and vegetable processors as well as a chemical company. Interchanging with CSX in Newark, the OMID transports freight on the former New York Central Hojack Line as well as the Pennsylvania Railroad's Elmira Branch. Like many of its neighboring short line railroads, the OMID maintains a small fleet of Alco diesel locomotives. The OMID's active roster consists of MLW M420 3560 and MLW RS-18 417.

The Ontario Midland traces its roots back to the mid-1850s when the Sodus Bay & Southern Railroad was organized in about 1853. Realizing the advantage of using Sodus Bay as a commercial port, local Sodus Point businessmen proposed construction of a dock for exporting and importing goods. By this time, the Canandaigua & Elmira Railroad was busy providing passenger and freight services on their rail network. Colonel Elias Cook, a civil engineer who built the Sodus Piers, took up the contract to build the Sodus Bay and Southern Railroad to meet the Canandaigua & Elmira Railroad at Stanley only a few miles southwest of Geneva. The Sodus Bay & Southern was organized due to recognition of the increasing demand for coal. However, constructing the railroad turned out to be more difficult than originally thought. The planning and early phases of the construction of the SB&S encountered many setbacks before collapsing due to insufficient funds. Twenty years worth of delays would follow the project's collapse before it could be refinanced and completed by a second contractor. The Sodus Bay & Southern officially began operations in July 1872, which immediately created a newfound access to the area, fully enhancing its commercial, industrial, and residential development. Shortly after the opening of the SB&S in the fall of that same year, the Northern Central Railroad purchased the Canandaigua & Elmira.

The first few years of Sodus Bay & Southern's operation were relatively unprofitable and were plagued by poor management. During the 1870s, Sylvanus J. Macy built and operated a bank near the west end of Sodus Bay and began supporting a variety of the financial needs of the area. The location of the bank became known as Macyville and eventually became the site of a railroad station, the malthouse of E. B. Parsons, and the coal trestle. Edward Harriman, the son-in-law of Averell Harriman of the banking and railroad family of Ogdensburg, arrived at Sodus Point in 1881. Together, Harriman and Macy, as well as other associates, purchased the struggling SB&S with plans to sell it to the Northern Central or the New York Central after improving the railroad's facilities and right of way. Three years later in 1884, Harriman sold the Sodus Bay & Southern to the Northern Central. This deal would mark the beginning of his career as a railroad baron, and he soon left the area to begin his heavy involvement in both the Union Pacific and the Southern Pacific Railroads.

Beginning in 1886, the Northern Central commenced construction of the first coal loading pier at Macyville as well as shipping coal from Pennsylvania at Sodus Point. This was only the beginning for Macyville as the area quickly began to develop as a major industrial center for Sodus Bay. Macyville quickly became a home for numerous ice houses, E. B. Parson's malthouse, and the Northern Central's station and switching yards. The malthouse complex consisted of four large grain storage elevators and a loading pier with tracks just north of the coal trestle. The coal trestle was built as a small, heavily constructed dock that was 400 feet long and stood 40 feet above the water. Two tracks sat on top of the coal trestle and stretched to its outer end with two coal pockets under each set of rails. Coal would be dumped from coal hoppers into these coal pockets before being manually dumped into the cargo holds of the many ships and freighters that traversed the great lakes. When a ship arrived, a coal hopper was positioned over the top of a pocket and the hatch doors at the bottom of the hopper car were opened to allow coal to drop into the pocket and run down the chute into the cargo holds of a waiting ship. In the cove of the harbor northeast of the coal trestle, another shipping pier for railroad cars and their cargos to be transferred onto ships was opened. The town docks that were located in this particular area were within walking distance of the foot of Bay Street where it meets Sand Point. Passenger steamers regularly brought in loads of people looking to enjoy their vacation in the area and the railroad's connection to Sodus Point also attracted more settlers and vacationers to the area. The Northern Central also set out to rebuild the entire line during the late 1880s. Heavier rail was installed, and wooden bridges were replaced with stronger structures made of iron. On top of that, the coal pier at Sodus Point was enlarged in 1894. By this point, passenger traffic was supported by four passenger trains daily in each direction from Elmira to Sodus Point.

The Northern Central was merged into the Pennsylvania Railroad in 1913 on a ninety-nine-year lease agreement. As a result of this merger, this particular line became the Elmira Branch that it is still referred to as today. The Elmira Branch once again went through a series of upgrades during the 1920s when the Pennsylvania Railroad installed heavier 130-pound rails, laying down stone ballast, and replaced iron bridges with steel versions. The coal trestle was also replaced with a newer one between 1927 and 1928, and the switching yard was expanded in order to increase the railroad's capabilities and keep up with the increasing demand for coal. Despite the effects of the Great Depression in the 1930s, the demand for coal continued to increase and it quickly became the main traffic source for the Elmira Branch. While coal revenues kept increasing, passenger travel by rail was steadily decreasing at the same time with public transportation now being provided by the roads via the automobile.

The coal business once again took a major jump when the Oswego power plant began receiving coal that was tariffed to move through Sodus Point and be loaded into freighters for the 30-mile trip east on Lake Ontario. During the World War II era, the Elmira Branch and the coal trestle at Sodus Bay saw large amounts of coal shipped to all points on Lake Ontario. During these few years, it was not unheard of to see two freighters loading up at the coal trestle while several more were anchored in the bay waiting their turn to receive their coal loads. Coal traffic on the branch saw another surge in the 1950s which resulted in another enlargement of the local switching yard. At its peak, the yard had room for 1,237 forty-five-foot coal hopper cars which is enough to assemble a train more than ten miles long. To compensate for loading bottlenecks, the pier's loading chutes and equipment were enlarged and upgraded. Mechanical shakers were added to the pier in 1956 which reduced the number of crew members needed to operate the dock by three or four less people. During 1957, in a season lasting about nine months, 2.5 million tons of coal were shipped from the Sodus coal trestle, shattering the record of 2.1 million tons from the 1951 season.

While the Pennsylvania Railroad transported massive amounts of coal from the state of Pennsylvania to the coal trestle at Sodus Point, the baton was passed to the great lakes freighters of Canadian Steamship Lines to move the coal to various points on Lake Ontario. The coal that they shipped was bituminous, which was dusty and dirty compared to the anthracite coal that most people used to heat their homes at the time. One of the most frequent visitors to the coal trestle was the self-unloading freighter known as the *Fontana*. For more than twenty years, the 400-foot-long *Fontana* spent most of her time sailing between Sodus Point and Oswego, carrying approximately 4,500 tons of coal each trip. For the *Fontana*, an average round trip between Sodus Point and Oswego took about fourteen to sixteen hours. The *Fontana* placed more than a million tons of coal in Oswego in a single season, making more than 250 round trips during that time. In terms of maximum cargo capacity, the *Fontana* held the equivalent of eighty to ninety hopper cars of coal, totaling out a season's delivery to the Oswego power plant at 21,000 carloads. This required the Pennsylvania Railroad to run one eighty-car train per day from the coalfields of Pennsylvania to Sodus Point for the full length of the shipping season just to meet the requirements for the Oswego plant alone. Other seafaring visitors to Sodus Point included the Bayfax, Coalfax, Midland Prince, Calcite, and the Stadocona. Overall, these ships accounted for 60 percent of coal tonnage shipped from the Sodus Point coal trestle.

Demand for coal remained strong from the late 1950s through 1963, even when the Erie-Lackawanna secured the coal delivery contract to Oswego. However, this change was accompanied by a significant decrease in the use of coal by industries around Lake Ontario as well as their conversion to oil and other sources of fuel and energy. In only four years, coal traffic from Sodus Point was reduced to zero. On December 11, 1967, the coal trestle was shut down by the Penn Central after the final freighter was loaded. This effectively spelled the end for the Elmira Branch and an era of long and heavy Pennsylvania Railroad coal drags to Lake Ontario had come to an end. It did not take long for the tracks to Sodus Point to fall into a state of disuse and disrepair. The only pleasing factor for the residents of Sodus Bay was the absence of the sound of the trestle shakers. After being unused for about three years, a local businessman purchased the property the coal trestle stood on with plans of dismantling it and using the lower section as a marina with slips for pleasure boats. In about three weeks, the dismantling of the coal trestle had made significant progress.

However, in a sad twist of fate, the coal trestle would burn to the ground on November 5, 1971. It was a windy day for the men working on the trestle at the time. While the men were working with acetylene torches near the outer end of the coal trestle, a red-hot bolt dropped onto a piece of timber covered in coal dust; it ignited a fire that destroyed what remained of the trestle. Despite this unfortunate incident, demolition work continued, and the former site of the Sodus Point coal trestle is now the site of a local marina. What started as a small humble coal dock that later expanded to a large coal trestle and became a local industrial staple now serves Sodus Point's economy as a marina. Meanwhile, the remaining remnants of the Elmira Branch continue to serve New York's economy as part of the Finger Lakes Railway at the south end as well as the Ontario Midland at the north end.

While the Ontario Midland operates on the former Elmira branch between Newark and Sodus, NY, the railroad also operates on the former New York Central Hojack Line from Sodus to Williamson, NY. The Hojack Line began as a branch line for the Rome, Watertown, and Ogdensburg Railroad that ran for approximately 150 miles along the southern shore of Lake Ontario from Oswego to Niagara Falls, New York. When it comes to how the Hojack Line got its name, it is fair to say that its exact origin is mostly unknown with many drawing their own theories. Attempts have been made to determine its official origin over the years. However, those attempts have resulted in little to no success. One such theory states that in the early days of the RW&O, a farmer in his backboard drawn by a mule was caught on a crossing when a train was approaching. When the mule was halfway across the tracks, the mule simply stopped. With the train drawing closer, the farmer got excited and began shouting, "Ho-Jack, Ho-Jack!" Amused by this incident, the railroad men began calling their line the "Ho-Jack." Another theory claims that Hojack originated from an engineer on one of railroad's trains, who was known as Jack Welch. Before the railroad, Welch used to be a farmer and was more familiar with horses and other animals than he was with steam locomotives. Whenever he stopped a train, he would shout "Whoa Jack!" In addition to that, another separate theory states that in the early years, railroad workers referred to each other when they wanted to hail to someone as "Hey Jack!" or "Ho Jack!"

The Hojack Line got its start in 1858 when the Lake Ontario Shore Railroad was chartered to build track from Oswego to Niagara Falls. The Lake Ontario Shore later became bankrupt and was absorbed into the RW&O in 1875. With the acquisition of the Lake Ontario Shore, the RW&O now had a through route from Niagara Falls to Norwood where connections to the Atlantic Ocean were available. However, the traffic was simply not present to help maintain the line and the RW&O quickly ran into financial trouble. During this time, two men fought each other for control of the RW&O: Samuel Sloan and Charles Parsons. With his background consisting of the Lackawanna, Sloan ran the RW&O rather poorly; Parsons, a New Englander, helped solve many of the problems that plagued the RW&O with assistance from Henry M. Britton. Together, they extended the road a few miles from Norwood to Massena in order to connect with the Grand Trunk that led into Montreal. On top of that, a direct line from Syracuse to Oswego was built, the roadbed and bridges were improved, and an extension to Rochester was also built. Around the same time the RW&O was expanding, another railroad was built from Utica, NY, to the North Country. Incorporated in 1852 by residents of Utica who were upset with Rome being the gateway to the St. Lawrence, the Utica & Black River Railroad connected villages and cities such as Boonville, Lowville, and Carthage. From Carthage, the railroad went to Clayton and Ogdensburg in one direction and to Sackets Harbor and Watertown in the other direction. In 1886, the U&BR merged into the RW&O.

Now with the prospect of the Fitchburg Railroad connecting to the RW&O, the New York Central organized the Mohawk & St. Lawrence Railroad with the intention to build to Watertown. This connection of only approximately 70 miles was required to connect with another neighboring railroad: The Boston, Hoosac Tunnel & Western, with either Utica or Rome, giving this Boston-based company direct access to Lake Erie. Naturally, the New York Central Railroad did not like this idea. In an effort to avoid another West Shore debacle, banking interests made arrangements to initiate talks between Parsons and the Vanderbilts. Ultimately deciding not to compete, they made a deal in 1891 to have the RW&O be leased to the New York Central. Despite obtaining control of a railroad in a non-competitive area, the New York Central paid a considerably high price for the RW&O. This lease agreement angered the citizens of Watertown since they felt that they were losing "their" railroad. In response, the New York Central initiated a public relations campaign with Chauncey Depew to gain public support from Watertown's citizens that all the incoming changes would be for the better. The new division headquarters was established in Watertown and the timetables still had the RW&O name incorporated into them. With sleeper cars running to the Thousand Islands and service improving, the New York Central's general passenger agent, George H. Daniels, went to work on the railroad's advertising and built the Thousand Islands up as a premier resort area. Going into the 1950s, most of the RW&O remained in service with everything east of Oswego becoming part of the St. Lawrence Division. By 1961, the St. Lawrence Division was merged into the Mohawk Division and the old Lake Ontario Shore Railroad was a part of the Syracuse Division. Today, the Ontario Midland has utilized the remnants of the Hojack Line and the Elmira Branch to provide rail service to local industries since 1979. In September 2022, the Livonia, Avon & Lakeville Railroad acquired the controlling stake in the railroad by purchasing 55% of its stock according to paperwork filed with the Surface Transportation Board, making the railroad the newest member to the LA&L family alongside the Bath & Hammondsport and Western New York & Pennsylvania Railroads.

Right: The Ontario Midland Railroad's company logo.

Below: After picking up their southbound cars in Williamson, OMID 3560 begins the journey to the CSX interchange in Newark.

OMID 3560 is an MLW M420W that was originally built for Canadian National in 1976. Before arriving in Sodus in 2022, the old product of Montreal Locomotive Works worked on the West Tennessee Railroad.

OMID 3560 passes a line of old railroad equipment being stored in a siding in Williamson. Notable pieces of equipment include a former G&W Alco diesel switcher and a pair of snow plows.

Sodus, New York, is the main base of operations for the Ontario Midland Railroad.

After diverging off the New York Central Hojack Line at the wye in Sodus, OMID 3560 leads its southbound train down the north end of the former Pennsylvania Railroad Elmira Branch.

Just north of Newark, the curve located at Heidenreich Road is one of the main photo locations that is popular with photographers looking to get a quality photo of the Ontario Midland Railroad in operation.

The Ontario Midland Railroad interchanges with CSX in Newark. OMID 3560 enters the small junction to drop off their southbound consist and pick up cars to take back north.

Running long hood forward northbound, OMID 3560 leads a small cut of covered hoppers and reefers to Sodus and Williamson.

The OMID crew sets out a pair of reefers at one of the railroad's customers: Sodus Cold Storage Inc.

Using a former Conrail caboose as a buffer car, OMID 3560 leads a loaded tanker filled with ethanol back to Sodus.

A former G&W Alco diesel switcher sits in a deadline of stored railroad equipment in Williamson.

OMID 3560 rolls past the local Motts factory in Williamson.

OMID 3560 departs the CSX interchange in Newark.

5

Rochester & Southern and Genesee & Wyoming: The Birthplace of a Short Line Conglomerate

Extending from urban Rochester, New York, to the rural landscapes of Western New York State under Genesee & Wyoming ownership, the Rochester and Southern Railroad is considered to be the line that launched the big short line conglomerate. Owning more than 100 properties and short line railroads worldwide, the G&W quickly expanded from a small upstate New York short line to the international transportation company it is today. Operating between the cities of Rochester, Dansville, and Silver Springs, this short line railroad interchanges with CSX at CP-373 on the Rochester Subdivision and at Genesee Junction on the West Shore Subdivision. The R&S also interchanges with the Livonia, Avon, and Lakeville Railroad at Genesee Junction in Rochester as well as Norfolk Southern via their Southern Tier Line in Silver Springs. Despite being a common sight on the Rochester and Southern Railroad and New York State itself, one can now easily find themselves watching orange and black diesel locomotives hauling large amounts of freight in every corner of the United States with the trademark G&W style logo being shown off with pride.

For clarification, there is difference between the Genesee & Wyoming Railroad and the Genesee & Wyoming Corporation. They are indeed related, but not exactly the same thing as one might think at first glance. The G&W Railroad was a small short line railroad that operated between Retsof and Caledonia, New York, on only 14.5 miles of track. Beginning in 1894, the railroad's main source of traffic was salt. The discovery of oil in Pennsylvania in 1859 encouraged people to search for more deposits of this natural resource in Western New York. However, a team drilling in the Genesee Valley found a large deposit of rock salt instead. When geologist Carrol Coker learned of this discovery, he managed to convince financier William Foster to invest in his venture. With Foster's financial assistance, a salt mine was opened in the vicinity of what is recognized as the largest rock salt deposit in the free world. By the early 1890s, the small community of Retsof was established around the entrance to the salt mine in honor of the man who had invested in its future. Retsof is William Foster's name spelled backwards.

As Livingston County's salt industry continued to grow, getting the product to market became a problem. While there were numerous railroad lines in the area, a link connecting Retsof to those railroad lines was needed. In order to solve this problem, the Genesee & Wyoming Valley Railroad was organized in 1891. The first stretch of the railroad's tracks ran from the salt mine to Retsof and connected with the Western New York and Pennsylvania Railway company which was later called the Rochester–Hinsdale, New York, branch of the Pennsylvania Railroad. This first stretch became known as the east branch. The G&W established a connection with the Delaware, Lackawanna, and Western when the G&WV purchased right of way and extended its tracks from Retsof to Greigsville. Later in 1894, the G&WV connected with the Lehigh Valley and the Buffalo, Rochester, and Pittsburgh, later known as the Rochester-East Salamanca branch of the B&O's Buffalo Division. By April 1895, the G&WV was transporting rock salt from Retsof to four interchange points on different railroads. By this time, the salt mine had been purchased by the Fuller family of Scranton, Pennsylvania, who had a keen interest in acquiring control of the railroad. When the salt mine was closed temporarily, the G&WV went into receivership and a Fuller family associate ended up being the receiver. As a result, the bankrupt railroad was purchased for the family this associate represented. In March 1899, the G&WV was officially reorganized as the Genesee & Wyoming Railroad and has been in operation since. To improve its services to their passengers and industrial customers in the area, the G&W added nine steam locomotives and one passenger coach to its holdings.

Cuylerville's Sterling Salt Company, owned by the International Salt Company, built its own short line railroad in 1908 to connect with the G&W at Retsof due to the company's preference of not having to rely on the Western New York & Pennsylvania Railroad. Fearing for the loss of business, the Pennsylvania Railroad claimed that the G&W was a switching railroad instead of a carrier, and as such was not permitted to extend through rates on any kind of commodity. As expected, legal action was quickly taken. When the case finally came up before the Supreme Court, the final decision favored the G&W, effectively declaring it to be a class two common carrier railroad. The primary purpose of the G&W was to transport rock salt from the Retsof mine to the railroad's interchange points. The salt was shipped not only to chemical plants in the Niagara Falls-Buffalo area and the East Coast, but also for the salt to be used by highway departments for melting snow and ice in various parts of the United States.

By 1920, the G&W was still operating on seventeen miles of track and gross revenue had risen to almost $500,000 with net income being reported at just above $270,000. Despite this period of prosperity, the G&W experienced a depression between 1922 and 1932 with revenues falling each year. By this point, net income dropped as low as $30,000. However, despite this financial slump, the railroad continued its tradition of paying quarterly dividends. In the decades that followed, the G&W prospered once again with annual revenues passing the million-dollar mark in 1955 and two million in 1970. The company's main office eventually moved to Clarks Summit, Pennsylvania, and operating revenues and net income increased again to $3.3 million and $662,000 respectively in 1978.

The G&W's expansion as a corporation had nowhere to go but up in the second half of the twentieth century. Mortimer B. Fuller III, the great-grandson of the founder, purchased a controlling interest in the G&W in 1977 and set out to obtain contracts from multiple industries that would make the railroad its sole supplier. Under his leadership, he renamed the G&W to Genesee & Wyoming Industries, Inc. and moved the company's main office to Greenwich, Connecticut. On top of that, the G&W quickly entered the rail-car leasing business and also began making many railway line purchases around the country. This would quickly propel the new GWI to become a leading provider of short line and regional rail transportation. While GWI was undergoing its expansion, the American railroad industry was going through significant changes after the United States government passed a 1980 federal act that deregulated the pricing and types of services that were provided by the railroads. The larger railroads of the time began focusing their management and resources on their long-haul core systems and sold off branch lines that were deemed unprofitable or were no longer considered cost effective to maintain or operate. Smaller railroad companies such as the short line railroads purchased these branch lines as they were more willing to commit the resources needed to meet the needs of customers that populated these railroad lines. GWI was no exception and began acquiring such railroad lines in 1985.

Not only was GWI expanding its rail network, the company was also expanding its geographic scope. In 1987, GWI purchased a portion of the Southern Pacific and named it the Louisiana & Delta Railroad. Roughly six years later in 1993, GWI purchased the Willamette & Pacific Railroad from Southern Pacific. Taking a similar approach to the unification of the A&E, B&P, and R&S, GWI began operations of the Portland & Western Railroad in 1995 on tracks leased from the Southern Pacific. By this point in the final years of the twentieth century, GWI had expanded its reach in just about every corner of the United States. The Genesee & Wyoming's rail network expanded beyond domestic operations in 1997 when it took on a 47.5-percent interest in a Canadian company that operated two short line railroads in Canada. Adding to their international expansion, GWI also purchased freight railroad assets of Australian National, a railroad company owned by Australia's federal government. Operating on approximately 900 miles of track, Australian National was renamed to Australia Southern Railroad.

Genesee & Wyoming Industries Inc. was renamed to Genesee & Wyoming Inc. in 1995. G&W's domestic railroad operations served more than 300 customers in 1997, the largest of them all being Commonwealth Edison, which accounted for about fifteen percent of the G&W's revenue for that year. Among the many commodities that the G&W hauled, coal, coke, and ores were the largest commodity group transported in 1997. Other commodities handled by the G&W included metals, pulp and paper, lumber, forest products, petroleum products, agricultural products, minerals and stone, chemicals, autos, and auto parts. In the modern twenty-first century, the G&W continues to make millions in revenue providing rail services for not only the United States, but for the world.

While slowly clearing Genesee Junction, a trio of B&P SD40-2s depart Rochester southbound on their way to Silver Springs. Genesee Junction serves as the Rochester & Southern's interchange with the Livonia Avon & Lakeville Railroad as well as CSX.

Heading southbound through Pavilion, B&P SD40M-2 3063 leads the road train to Silver Springs where the railroad interchanges freight traffic with Norfolk Southern.

When GWI acquired the Allegheny & Eastern Railroad in 1992, the A&E, B&P, and R&S virtually became one railroad with shared customer service, dispatching tasks, and pooled power. For example, it is not uncommon to find B&P locomotives operating R&S road trains such as GW-1, RS-1, and BL-1.

Pittsburgh & Lehigh Junction, also known as P&L Junction, was the G&W's primary interchange point that allowed the 14.5-mile railroad to provide advantageous shipping options for the salt the railroad transported. The salt could travel to customers via the Lehigh Valley, New York Central, Erie, or the Buffalo, Rochester & Pittsburgh (later Baltimore & Ohio) railroads.

Right: When it comes to motive power, the R&S is home to a variety of first and second generation EMD diesel locomotives hauling long trains of salt hoppers as well as mixed freight for numerous customers that populate the railroad's small network.

Below: Battling the uphill grade into Warsaw, B&P SD40M-2's 3064 and 3063 begin the last stretch of their southbound journey to Silver Springs. The train works its way up the hill past the derelict depot and a pair of old Erie Railroad boxcars.

The R&S reached Buffalo in 1991 via a connection at Silver Springs, New York, with Canadian Pacific (now Norfolk Southern) and was operating on sixty six miles of track in the Rochester, New York, area by 1997. This was also the time when the G&W acquired the Buffalo & Pittsburgh Railroad from the Pennsylvania division of CSX. Upon acquiring the B&P, which became one of GWI's biggest properties, the B&P had 279 miles of track.

R&S GW-1 rounds the bend on the final approach to Silver Springs.

Highballing southbound out of Le Roy, B&P 3063 leads the train towards Pavilion.

The tracks of the Rochester & Southern cross over the Oatka Creek in Le Roy as well as in Scottsville.

After interchanging with Norfolk Southern in Silver Springs, B&P SD40-2 3331 leads the road train back north to Rochester.

While the former BR&P and B&O trackage still remains in good condition with G&W and R&S today, the depot in Warsaw has definitely seen better days.

Above: R&S 2030 is one of only a small handful of diesel units that wear the R&S lettering on the railroad's roster. A majority of their power sports the Buffalo & Pittsburgh lettering.

Right: B&P 3063 kicks up some dust as the southbound road train approaches Warsaw.

The southbound road train begins to slow down as it approaches P&L Junction in Caledonia.

B&P 3103 and R&S 2030 pass by the Scottsville depot while on their way southbound to Dansville.

R&S BL-1 departs Rochester southbound.

For a railroad company that started out with less than fifteen miles of track, the G&W directly interchanged with an impressive number of larger railroads during its history. The G&W directly interchanged with: Lehigh Valley, Erie, DL&W, Pennsylvania Railroad, New York Central, BR&P, Baltimore & Ohio, Chessie System, Delaware & Hudson, Penn Central, Erie-Lackawanna, Conrail, and CSX.

After clearing P&L Junction, the southbound BL-1 picks up speed as it rumbles past a local grain mill just outside of Retsof.

Picking up some covered hopper cars to be taken south to Dansville, BL-1 switches the sidings in Retsof.

GWI began their railroad line acquisition spree by purchasing the neighboring Danville & Mt. Morris Railroad, a small railroad headquartered in Leicester, New York, with eight miles of track running south of G&W's own right of way. One year later in 1986, GWI acquired the Ashford Junction-Rochester line from CSX.

Before GWI purchased the Rochester & Southern Railroad, the R&S was losing money and in terrible condition at the time due to lack of maintenance. As a result of this deferred maintenance, the threat of a derailment forced trains to operate at very slow speeds as well as limit the amount of traffic the railroad could carry with any train operating on their tracks.

CANADIAN PACIFIC
CP
BPRR
3103

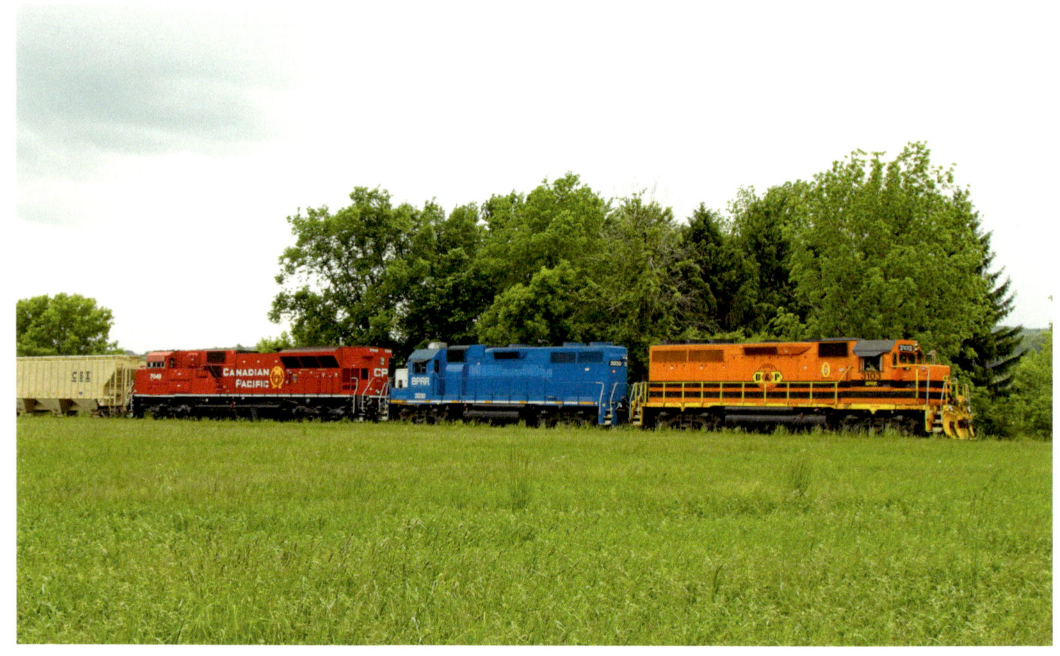

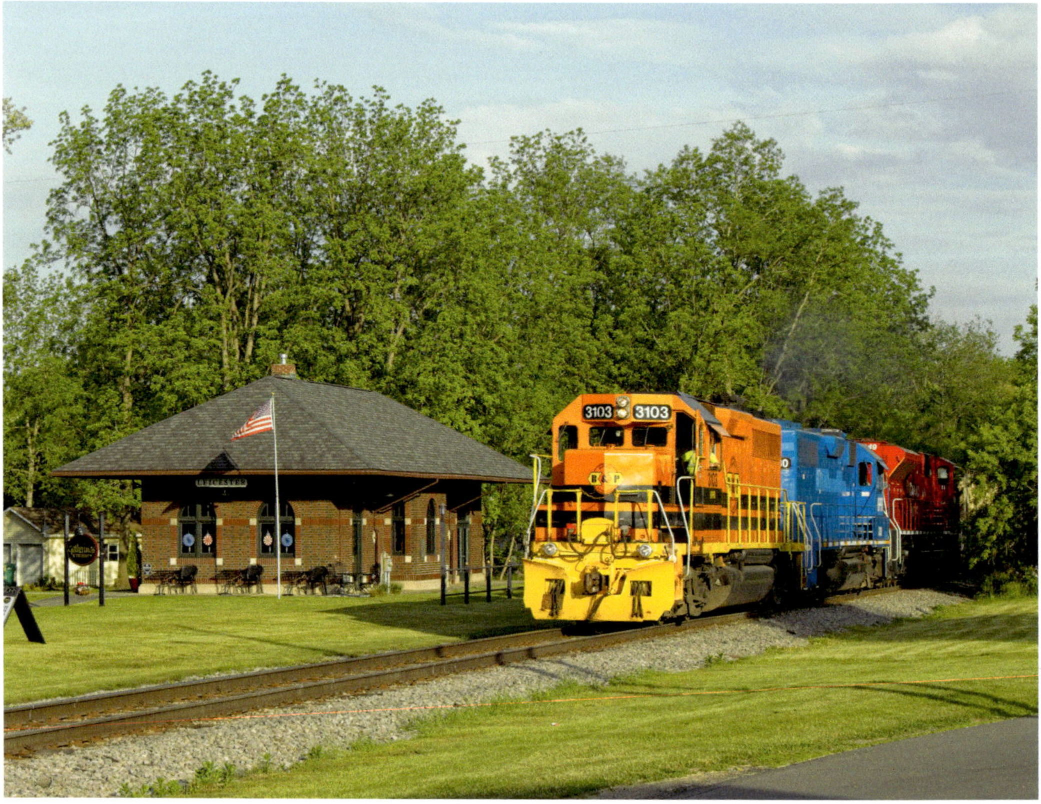
3103
3103
B&P

Heading southbound through Retsof, the R&S BL-1 job leads a Canadian National SD70M-2 and a line of hoppers bound for AMP in Dansville.

Opposite above: Located at the end of the line in Dansville on the former Dansville & Mt. Morris trackage, American Motive Power (AMP) is one of the Rochester & Southern's main customers. Ferrying a wide variety of diesel locomotives from multiple railroads for repairs or overhauls between Rochester and Dansville is a common sight on the railroad's BL-1 job.

Opposite below: Under the ownership of G&W, the R&S saw many improvements which allowed revenue carloads to increase by thirty-six percent between 1986 and 1988 and a grand total of thirty-nine customers by 1989, one of them being Eastman Kodak Co.

The Bath & Hammondsport Railroad: The Railroad That Regained Its Independence

Nestled in the Finger Lakes Region of New York State, the Bath & Hammondsport Railroad Company was originally a small independent short line that operated on nine miles of track between its namesake cities. The B&H ran between Hammondsport, at the head of Keuka Lake, and Bath, where it connected with the Erie Railroad. However, in modern times, the B&H is vastly different than what it was decades prior. For those living in the twenty-first century, the B&H now operates regular freight services between Cohocton and Painted Post, NY, using ALCO diesel locomotives that are commonly found on the B&H's parent company, the Livonia, Avon & Lakeville Railroad, as well as the Western New York & Pennsylvania Railroad. The original B&H still connects with the modern B&H in Bath, NY with a small section of the original line recently returned to active service in 2023. The story of the Bath & Hammondsport Railroad is a story about a small short line railroad that began as an independent entity, was briefly absorbed into the Erie Railroad, and later regained its independence.

In the middle of the nineteenth century, interest in building a railroad in the Bath and Hammondsport, New York, areas began to surface when the Buffalo, Corning & New York Railroad's tracks reached Bath. Keuka Lake, one of the Finger Lakes, had already established itself as a method of transportation and travel due to it being connected to Seneca Lake by the Crooked Lake Canal since being completed in 1833. At this point in time, Seneca Lake was already connected to the Erie Canal via the Seneca & Cayuga Canal, which had already been opened in 1828. The Crooked Lake Canal's official opening coincided with the incorporation of Penn Yan, New York, as a village. Thanks to the Canandaigua & Elmira Railroad, Penn Yan got its first railroad in 1851. The Canandaigua & Elmira became one of three railroads that were operated by the New York & Erie Railroad which already had established a route between Elmira and the Suspension Bridge near Niagara Falls. Another railroad, known as the Sodus Bay, Corning & Southern Railroad, ran from Penn Yan to a connection with the Erie Railroad in Savona, New York, after being incorporated in 1871. The connection at Savona was approximately six miles south of Bath. Preliminary grading was then carried out by the Sodus Bay, Corning & Southern as well as two succeeding railroad companies. One of them was the Penn Yan, Lake Keuka & Southern which was incorporated in 1899. Grading would eventually continue from Savona to Bradford, New York, but even then, Penn Yan had a railroad while Hammondsport still had nothing as of 1871.

In January 1872, Hammondsport finally punched its ticket into the railroad world when the Bath & Hammondsport Railroad received a charter from the State of New York to construct a three-foot narrow-gauge line between its namesake cities with an authorized capitalization of $700,000. Additionally, the B&H was also authorized to construct a railroad route from Bath to Hornellsville. However, this never came to fruition. C. D. Champlin of Hammondsport assumed the position of president of the railroad and the line was officially completed in June 1875. The celebration of the completion of the B&H was combined with the celebration of America's ninety-ninth year of independence on July 5, 1875, amid a significantly large amount of fanfare. Festivities that were included in the combined celebration in Hammondsport included a ninety-nine-gun salute, a parachute jump from the steeple of the Presbyterian Church, band concerts, and fireworks. Two steamships conducted numerous excursions on Keuka Lake while the B&H operated hourly services during the day. Bath's celebrations occurred in a similar fashion only two days prior.

The Bath & Hammondsport's tracks were re-laid to standard gauge in 1889 which inevitably forced the railroad to shut down for six months in order to complete the project. The late 1800s would prove to be the "glory days" for the B&H. In 1892, the Lake Keuka Navigation Company absorbed the Crooked Lake Navigation Company. This takeover helped bring a large number of steamboat operations under one flag. At this point in the nineteenth century, Charles W. Drake was president of both the B&H and the Lake Keuka Navigation Company by the mid-1890s. As a result of Drake's ownership in both companies, there were boat-train connections for both directions listed in the railroad and the boat company schedules. Sometimes excursion traffic would become so heavy that equipment would have to be borrowed from the neighboring Kanona & Prattsburg Railroad. To make accommodations for this particular arrangement, the B&H and K&P obtained limited running rights over the Erie Railroad between Bath and Kanona.

The B&H would lose its independence as a railroad in 1908 when the Erie Railroad began acquiring shares of the B&H. Under the administration of Erie Railroad president Frederick Underwood, the Erie was interested in the B&H's operations due to the railroad's grape and wine business which they believed could be expanded. To help expand the B&H's grape and wine business, grape specialist F. W. Gristock of Penn Yan was appointed by the Erie as a commercial agent in Hammondsport. On top of that, the Erie planned to build a warehouse and dock facilities to handle the new business. Two freighters, the *Rochester* and *Elmira*, were also added to the Lake Keuka Navigation Company's fleet of boats. Prior to obtaining control of the B&H, the Erie purchased the Lake Keuka Navigation Company in 1906. The *Rochester* and *Elmira* were built as flat bottom vessels with gasoline engines to transport freight traffic. Despite being built to transport freight, the Rochester and Elmira did carry passengers. This operation saw lots of success up until approximately World War I. Due to the entrance of the automobile and how quickly Americans took to the roads, steamboat traffic rapidly declined with steamboat services ending at the end of 1917. Despite the disappearance of the steamboats, passenger services on the B&H continued into the 1920s. The freighter boats disappeared from Keuka Lake when they were sold in 1919. While most of the freight business was lost to the trucks, some of it continued on Keuka Lake for a few more years. Another devastating blow that was dealt to the B&H was the passing of the Volstead Act in 1919 which ushered in the Prohibition Era, curtailing the wine and liquor business. As a result of this sharp decrease in freight traffic, the B&H found itself struggling to survive going into the Great Depression. Motive power on the B&H was considered to be worn out and the remaining business did not justify the need to acquire more modern equipment. Between 1913 and 1926, the Erie brought in a group of older 2-8-0 steam locomotives that were built in the 1880s to handle the remaining traffic on the line.

After New York's Southern Tier experienced severe flooding that washed out part of the B&H line in July 1935, the Erie decided that enough was enough with losing money through the B&H and put the line up for abandonment. The Interstate Commerce Commission gave the Erie permission in August of that same year. A group of businessmen from Hammondsport stepped forward with an offer to take over operations on the B&H and the arrangements were made with the Erie in May 1936. On top of receiving the Erie's blessing, the new organization was given a 4-6-0 steam locomotive that was leased from the Erie. Operations on the B&H resumed in July of 1936 after one year of rebuilding the line. To celebrate the re-birth of the B&H, the railroad organized and operated the "Wine Special" which carried 100 invited railroad officials from Bath to the Glenwood Club in Hammondsport for what one journalist described as "a prolonged session of wining and dining in the famed Hammondsport tradition."

Beginning in 1937, the new and independent Bath & Hammondsport Railroad set to work on making more improvements and one of those was obtaining new motive power. For the B&H, the Erie Railroad ten-wheeler had proven to be too heavy to operate on the light rail that the B&H's route consisted of. The ten-wheeler was returned to the Erie in 1938 when the B&H had acquired what may be their most famous steam locomotive, 2-6-0 no. 11. After B&H acquired the locomotive from Rhode Island's Narragansett Pier Railroad, it became the mainstay locomotive of the railroad for over a decade. No. 11 was built in 1920 by the Cooke Works of the American Locomotive Company (Alco) in Paterson, New Jersey, and is a 2-6-0 "Mogul" type that was one of fifty-four engines of four different wheel arrangements built between 1920 and 1925 for export to Cuba's sugar cane fields. After World War I, fluctuations in the world sugar markets reduced the demand for these engines which left a number of them unsold on the factory floor. In order to sell these new steam locomotives, Alco turned to the short line railroad market. No. 11 was purchased by the Narragansett Pier Railroad in Peace Dale, Rhode Island, in 1923 and was immediately put to work on the eight-and-a-half-mile railroad. No. 11's tenure in Rhode Island lasted for fourteen years before it was replaced by a gas-mechanical locomotive in 1937. From 1937 until its retirement in 1949, no. 11 handled all the B&H freight business as well as the railroads passenger excursions. Today, the B&H Rail Corporation operates fifty-two miles of track from Wayland through Bath to Painted Post. As of 2023, a small portion of the original Bath & Hammondsport line has been reactivated to service a newly established customer in Bath while the section northeast of Bath remains out of service.

The modern B&H lettering as seen on the side of Alco C424 no. 422.

Beginning the day in Coopers Plains, the B&H crew run their Alco units south to grab their westbound train from the Norfolk Southern interchange in Painted Post.

The daily B&H train crosses the Cohocton River westbound with a line of tankers to be delivered to Inergy Midstream LCC in Savona.

LA&L 424 leads the westbound train through Campell, New York.

Right: Clearing Kanona and approaching Bath, LA&L 423 leads B&H 422 and four tank cars from Cohocton eastbound back to Painted Post.

Below: Running with one diesel unit on each end of their short train, the B&H crew continue their journey westbound to Cohocton.

With their work completed in Savona and Cohocton, B&H 422 leads the train back to Painted Post to interchange with Norfolk Southern.

The LA&L transferred operations to the Cohocton Valley Railroad Corporation, a LA&L subsidiary, in 2001. Not long afterward, the Cohocton Valley later got renamed to the Bath & Hammondsport Rail Corporation. The B&H Rail Corporation also leased from Norfolk Southern its ex-Erie Lackawanna line from Bath to Painted Post where the interchange of freight traffic takes place.

With switching in Painted Post almost complete, the pair of Alco C424s prepare to run back to Coopers Plains to finish their day of work.

Bath & Hammondsport no. 5, an Alco S-1 diesel switcher, sits on a siding in Cohocton in outdoor storage. Despite being exposed to the elements, the old S-1 appears to be in fairly good condition.

The B&H earned its nickname, "The Champagne Route," when the railroad began shipping out wine produced by the local wineries along with its typical freight traffic of outgoing produce, incoming coal, and general merchandise. The railroad's passenger services maintained connections with the New York, Lake Erie & Western in Bath as well as the Keuka Lake boats in Hammondsport, which allowed the railroad to operate excursions during the busy summer months.

In the 1990s, Stanley Clark, the president of the Champagne Railroad, created a dinner train that ran between Cohocton and the Taylor Winery outside of Hammondsport. While this train was operated by the Champagne Railroad, it was actually a separate subsidiary known as the Burgundy Champagne Railroad Inc. Since the BCR would not be involved in any other operations except for a recreational dinner train and was located only in New York State, it was not subject to the Interstate Commerce Commission's jurisdiction.

The BCR began operations in July 1994, but this increase in passenger traffic would be brief due to the passing of Stanley Clark in August 1995. As a result of his death, the BCR operation was discontinued.

Through both its careers on the Narragansett Pier and the B&H, no. 11 became a symbol of the American tradition of small independent railroads connecting local small communities to the national rail network. In 1949, the B&H retired no. 11 in favor of diesel of power. Having become an object of sentimental attachment, the B&H's owners would not sell the small mogul, fearing that it would be scrapped.

Left: Before being purchased by the Everett Railroad in 2006, no. 11 went through multiple owners between 1949 and 2006. Previous owners included Dr. Stanley A. Groman for his Rail City Museum in Sandy Pond, New York (1955), Dr. John P. Miller of the Narragansett Pier Railroad (1977), and the Middletown & New Jersey Railroad (1981).

Below: After an extensive restoration, no. 11 returned to service in the fall of 2015 for the first time since the 1970s and serves as the Everett Railroad's primary excursion locomotive.

While Conrail took many railroad lines over, the new railroad company was not obligated to keep all of them. Therefore, the portion of the Erie Lackawanna from Wayland to Kanona was sold to the Steuben County Industrial Development Authority (SCIDA). In April 1976, SCIDA chose the B&H to operate the recently purchased trackage which tripled the B&H's range of operations as a result.

Later on in February 1993, SCIDA would acquire all of the B&H assets with the exception of the trackage north of NY Route 54A and the property associated which was retained for real estate development. In March of that same year, SCIDA leased all of it to the Champagne Railroad which began operations only two days later. SCIDA also acquired the section of track between Kanona and Bath from Conrail. As a result, SCIDA owned a route from Wayland through Bath to Hammondsport.

The Livonia, Avon & Lakeville Railroad was chosen by SCIDA to be the new operator of the B&H in April of 1996 and the LA&L began operations in May of that year. A few months later in November, flooding from a storm caused severe damage to the line between Bath and Cohoctan. Fortunately for the B&H, LA&L and SCIDA received a FEMA grant to repair the line.

After servicing Liquid Products LLC, LA&L 424 passes through the old Birkett Mills facility in Cohocton, New York, with a tank car to be interchanged with Norfolk Southern in Painted Post.

Bibliography

"Bath & Hammondsport Railroad Company." Rail City Museum, www.railcitymuseum. com/RAI_CITY_v_04_02_2011/Bath_and_Hammondsport_RR.html.

Batzing, Dick. "The Hojack Line Story." *Friends of Webster Trails*, edited by Don Schaefer, www.webstertrails.org/hojack/story.php.

Berger, Eric. "Watco Launches Ithaca Central on Former Lehigh Valley Route." *Railfan & Railroad Magzine*, 14 Nov. 2018, railfan.com/watco-launches-ithaca-central-on-former-lehigh-valley-route/.

Burns, Adam. "Livonia, Avon & Lakeville Railroad Corporation." *American Rails*, 12 Mar. 2022, www.american-rails.com/lal.html.

Burns, Adam. "Penn Central Railroad: A Corporate Disaster." *American Rails*, 31 Mar. 2022, www.american-rails.com/pc.html

Conrail, conrail.com/about-conrail/history/.

"Everett Railroad ." *Hawkins Rails*, 19 June 2019, hawkinsrails.net/preservation/ev/ev_tourist.html.

Gable, Walt. "Looking Back: The Lehigh Valley railroads connecting Seneca County to Geneva." *Finger Lakes Times*, 24 June 2018, www.fltimes.com/lifestyle/looking-back-the-lehigh-valley-railroads-connecting-seneca-county-to-geneva/article_1e6f0a1c-b654-5f5b-8819-1a4d702e950e.html.

"Genesee & Wyoming Inc. History." Funding Universe, www.fundinguniverse.com/company-histories/genesee-wyoming-inc-history/.

"History." Lehigh Valley Railroad Historical Society, edited by Mike Roque, lvrrhs.org/history/index.htm.

Jackson, Ted. "Erie Railroad Rochester Division: Chapter Four." Rochester & Genesee Valley Railroad Museum, 23 Aug. 2020, www.rgvrrm.org/erie-railroad-rochester-division-chapter-four/.

Lawrence, Scot. Genesee & Wyoming Railroad, 15 June 2016, scotlawrence.github.io/GW/GWpage.html.

"Livonia, Avon & Lakeville No. 20." Rochester & Genesee Valley Railroad Museum, www.rgvrrm.org/about/railroad/lal20/.

Palmer, Richard F. "Old Number 11 and the Bath & Hammondsport Railroad." *The Crooked Lake Review*, Dec. 1994, www.crookedlakereview.com/articles/67_100/81dec1994/81palmer.html.

Palmer, Richard. "Where Did the Term "Hojack" Originate?", edited by Russel Nelson, 30 May 2006, russnelson.com/RWnO/origin-of-hojack.html.

Pinneo, Gary. "The Last Passenger Train from Penn Yan." Yates County History Center, Sept. 2008, www.yatespast.org/articles/lasttrain.html.

"Predecessor Railroads -- History of the Lines that Comprise Today's LAL." Livonia, Avon & Lakeville Railroad, web.archive.org/web/20081223231418/http:/www.lalrr.com/history.html.

"Rome, Watertown & Ogdensburg Railroad Company." Penny Vanderbilt and KC Jones: All About Railroads, penneyandkc.wordpress.com/rome-watertown-ogdensburg-railroad-company/.

Rothbart, Charles. "Railfanning Finger Lakes Railway's Geneva-Solvay Job." *Railpace Newsmagazine*, 15 Sept. 2020, railpace.com/railfanning-finger-lakes-railways-geneva-solvay-job/.

Shinal, Paul J. "Way Back When in Seneca County: Auburn Road one of the oldest rail lines." *Finger Lakes Times*, 29 May 2016, fltimes.com/lifestyle/way-back-when-in-seneca-county-auburn-road-one-of-the-oldest-rail-lines/article_281aba08-2368-11e6-9623-1b0a995a0681.html#:~:text=In%201850%2C%20the%20two%20Auburn,fr.

"Skaneateles Short Line Railroad ." Skaneateles Historical Society, Skaneateles Historical Society, 2023, skaneateleshistoricalsociety.org/short-line-railroad.

"The Sodus Point and Southern Railroad." *Abandoned Rails*, www.abandonedrails.com/sodus-point-and-southern-railroad.

"The Sodus Point Coal Trestle ." *Historic Sodus Point*, historicsoduspoint.com/commerce/railroad-and-coal-trestle/coal-trestle/.

Wilson, Les. "Livonia Avon & Lakeville Railroad." *The Greater Rochester Railfan Page*, 20 Feb. 2005